T0062508

Joys,
Fears,
And
Tears

Robert Elliott Cohen

iUniverse, Inc.
Bloomington

Joys, Fears, And Tears

iUniverse books may be ordered through booksellers or by contacting:

iUniverse
1663 Liberty Drive
Bloomington, IN 47403
www.iuniverse.com
1-800-Authors (1-800-288-4677)

ISBN: 978-1-4502-5188-4 (pbk)
ISBN: 978-1-4502-5189-1 (ebk)

Printed in the United States of America

iUniverse rev. date: 11/24/10

Table of Contents

1
I Have Wheels
By: Robert Cohen
Oct. 1994

I Have Wheels
I have wheels.
I have wheels and I can roll
I may never ride a bike,
But in my wheelchair, I go
Up the street,
Down the street,
Away I go.
I have wheels I can roll!

By: Robert Cohen

2
Light
Robert E. Cohen
July 26, 1998

Being light has its advantages because everyone has certain qualities that they like in the opposite sex and one of mine just happens to be lightness. Because I think there is something special in light females but I just can not quite put my finger on it maybe it's because it seems like they have brains and beauty all wrapped up in the one not saying that dark skin sisters do not have those things as well it's just that light skin express their brains and beauty in a unique way.

3
Sister
Robert E. Cohen
June 16, 1999

A sister is a unique black woman who is very
educated with high hopes for the future.
This extremely special sister's receives the
highest praise from everyone. A sister's
feelings are very important to someone like
me. Because the way I see it a sister should
be treated with the up most respect because
when a beautiful sister and a fine brother
get together it can be a very romantic thing
as long as one of you don't do anything
to mistreat the relationship however if
something happens a sister's feelings are
hurt a sister is ready to breakup with the
brother that is why I always treat my female
associates with up most honor and respect
because although I am single at the present
time I intend to be the most respectful
boyfriend that a girl could ever have.

The End

4
The Real World
Robert E. Cohen
June 19, 1999

The Real World is a cruel place where everyone has to look out for themselves because everywhere you go there is trouble and if you are not careful you could find yourself trapped in something that you cannot find your way out of. The Real World is also a place where anyone will do anything to make a dollar from selling drugs to kids to killing their own family members because when you are in the Real World it seems like everything is centered around money when actually it's not it is centered around the person and how the person acts because everybody is not out to be evil some are just misunderstood people who are crying out for attention and they don't have any other way to express themselves.

5
Racism
Robert E. Cohen
June 19, 1999

Racism is something that is used to stop
people of a certain color particularly blacks
from doing the things that other people can
do because people think that black people
will cause a ruckus and it is true because
every time that Savannah has something
for black people we go out and act like
fools so what can we expect people to think
when we prove them right time after time.

6
The Vision
Robert E. Cohen
June 20, 1999

The Vision is something that at first glimpse
is not clear because at first appearance it
is dark and the Vision sort of scares you.
You begin to move very slowly towards the
light and flip the light switch. You continue
to move slowly around the house until you
reach the broom. You grab the broom and
continue searching for the Vision because
you know that the ugly vision could show
its face at any given moment. Knowing this
your next place would be the bedroom. You
approach the door with caution very quietly
turn the knob and enter the room but find
nothing. You continue your search in the
bathroom. You hit the lights and there it
is. You start to hit it with the broom but
suddenly look again and see that it is only a
rubber band ball. You wasted all your energy
searching for the Vision and all along it
was nothing but a rubber band ball and you
think what a waste of a perfectly good day.

The End

7
Drugs
Robert E. Cohen
July 1, 1999

Drugs are a very addictive substance that
affects the mind and will make you act as
if you have no common sense because you
cannot make a wise choice when you are
under the influence because when you are
under the influence the alcohol controls you
instead of you controlling you .The alcohol
will make you do things that being sober
would not because when you get drunk it is
next to impossible to communicate with you.

8
Romance
Robert E. Cohen
July 1, 1999

Romance can be a very sweet compassionate
thing that a lot of people take lightly
because people think that romance is just
something that is there to say that you have
someone that truly cares about you but there
is more to it than that because once you are
committed to someone that begins a sacred
bond between you and that amazingly special
female that you are committed yourself
to. Once that bond has been broken it is
extremely difficult for the other person to
be able to ever trust you again and that is
the biggest mistake I made with the girl that
could be one of my closest friends and I am
sincerely sorry that it went down that way.

9
Independence Day
Robert E. Cohen
July 3, 1999

Independence Day is a historical day in the lives of all Americans all over the world because this was the day Americans won their independence from Great Britain. Oh what a glorious day it was when the Americans could finally claim their land from Great Britain because the people of Great Britain were power hungry control freaks who thought that they were all that and a bag of chips when actually they were nothing but scared people who did not want Americans to have any power or authority. But on July 4, 1776 that all changed because this day was when Americans celebrated their victory over Great Britain. They celebrated this glorious occasion with an event only to be identified as the Boston Tea Party. Hallelujah what a glorious day it was.

Peace and Love, America.
Increase the peace and erase the Hate.

10
The Black Girl II
Robert E. Cohen
July 5, 1999

The Black Girl is a very beautiful unique
young lady with the highest intelligence.
When she walks by all the guys stop
and stare because they have never seen
a more beautiful sight. She is treated
with the utmost respect because she
knows that she is "ALL THAT" and
no one can tell her anything because
she is Strong, Black, and Secure.

11
Happiness
Robert E. Cohen
July 5, 1999

Happiness is a very strong important
feeling that everyone has the pleasure
of experiencing at one point or another.
This feeling can occur when something
happens that makes you smile, when
someone expresses their feelings toward
you, when that one special person who you
admire most walks by. When someone else
is happy does it make you happy? When
you wake up in the morning and realize
that you still have warm blood flowing
through your veins? When you graduate
from high school or college? When you
win the lottery? When your birthday
comes and you become one year older?

12
The Delicate Flower
Robert E. Cohen
July 6, 1999
Inspiration: Nikia Hall

The Delicate Flower is a flower that should
be treated with extremely special care
because this is a very special flower that
is as beautiful as a bright morning star.
This extremely special flower is one that
has extremely high expectations and lots
of positive values about it because a flower
this beautiful deserves nothing less than the
utmost respect and courtesy by anyone that
it comes in contact with. If any differently
the delicate flower will feel hurt and
mistreated. This is why we should always
treat people as we would like to be treated.

Love Always,
Robert Elliott Cohen
        AKA
"The Reality Poet"

13
Attraction
Robert E. Cohen
July 7, 1999

An attraction is a serious feeling that occurs when a person sights another person and they cannot keep their eyes off that person. This is what is known as Attraction. When an attraction occurs it may take you a while to figure out that someone is attracted to you but you will eventually know because the person will send you signs that will inform you of this. However, there will be some cases where the person that you are attracted to may not share that same attraction. If this is the case, do not sweat it just remain friends and let nature take its course.

14
Kindness
Robert E. Cohen
July 8, 1999

Kindness is a very nice deed that if you
are not careful people will take your
kindness for weakness. When you are kind
to people only good things can happen
thus you will more than likely have a
more successful prosperous life. You will
communicate better with people when you
use kindness because when kindness is
used things can go down more smoothly.

15
Birth
Robert E. Cohen
July 9, 1999

A birth is a very glorious experience that will assist you in having a more joyful life with a lot of high points that you enjoy after the birth has occurred. Another thing about a birth is there are a lot of responsibilities to be taken care of. A lot of teenagers make the mistake of letting a birth happen before they are really prepared to care for a newborn. They are stuck without anyone to help them. So never make a birth before you are prepared.

16
Thanks
Robert E. Cohen
July 11, 1999

Give thanks to the Lord for letting you
see yet another day. Give thanks to those
who have helped you to become what
you are today. Give thanks to the person
who is always there for you through thick
and thin. Give thanks for the blessings
that God has bestowed upon you. Give
thanks for all that you have succeeded.

17
Sweetie
Robert E. Cohen
July 14, 1999

A SWEETIE is a very special person that
is not a girlfriend it is just a person that
you consider a really close friend that you
should be able to confide in about anything
no matter how delicate the situation may
be. Once you have found this wonderful lady
there should be nothing that comes between
you and that person. However, sometimes
things get twisted and you get messed up.
For example, the person that I consider
to be my SWEETIE right now she seems
to think that I am cheating on her which
could not be any further from the truth.

18
Emotions
Robert E. Cohen
July 16, 1999

Emotions are something that differ
between men and women. Some men
think that because they are men they are
not supposed to express their emotions
because of what other males will think of
them but they should not be concerned
with what other males think. Other males
cannot determine their salvation.
Women, on the other, are not afraid to
express their emotions because women cry
and it does not make a difference to them
who sees them show their emotions. That
is why I have such a difficult time trying to
figure out why men have a hard time showing
their emotions but I guess that is just one of
the differences between men and women.

19
Tears
Robert E. Cohen
July 17, 1999

Tears are very quiet things that are difficult
to detect unless you see a tear drop fall
from someone's eye you don't realize they
are crying. When you do realize they are
crying you spend the next few minutes
trying to calm the person down and figure
out what the situation is. The funny thing
about tears is you don't have a particular
reason for them some people just cry
because it makes you feels better.

20
The Crush
Robert E. Cohen
July 28, 1999
Dedication: Dashawna Hanshaw

A Crush is a very strong emotional feeling
that you feel towards someone who started
as an associate then as time goes on that
association evolves into a friendship. Then
the friendship turns into a liking and
the liking turns into a crush. You have a
difficult time confessing your feelings to the
person. You don't want to make a fool of
yourself so you try to find the calmest way
to tell the person without being detected.
Sometimes the person does not believe you
no matter how many times you tell them.

21
The Connection
Robert E. Cohen
August 3, 1999

A connection is a romantic way to find that
special someone that you are attracted
to. However, the connection is not
something you can rush because if you
rush a connection you will have a difficult
time trying to figure out whether or not
you are connecting with the right person.
Another conflict that you are likely to run
into by rushing a connection is whether
or not the person will treat you right
because when you begin a relationship
at first it seems like you and the person
are getting along nicely but if something
goes wrong not only is the connection
broken two hearts are also broken.
Do not rush it and you will be fine.

22
The Spirit
Robert E. Cohen
August 3, 1999
Dedication: Sarah Truly

The Spirit is something that God left us
when He died to assure us that we are
never out of his presence. When we are
in His presence no hurt, harm, or danger
can come upon us. He loves so much that
He even knows the exact number of hairs
on our heads. Now if He cares enough
about us to know the exact number of
hairs on our head don't you think that
He would care if you accept Him?

23
The African Queen
Robert E. Cohen
August 3, 1999

The African Queen is a queen of great
beauty, power, and is highly respected by
everyone that she comes in contact with
because she is the type who treats everybody
as equals. Just because she has power she
does not make anyone feel as if they are
lower than her. That is the way a real queen
should carry herself so that she can get
every blessing that God has in store for her.

24
The Special Friend
Robert E. Cohen
August 3, 1999

The Special Friend is someone who you are willing to do anything for and should be willing to do anything for you. The special friend is someone who is always there when you need them no matter what the situation may be because you are always there for them. That is what a good trusting friendship is built on.

25
Hope
Robert E. Cohen
August 4, 1999

Hope is something that everyone should
be able to experience at some point in life
because hope can get you a long way in life.
Without hope you cannot be as successful
as you would like to be in life. So as you
possibly see by now the hope that you have
inside of you will help to succeed and have a
more blessed and prosperous life on earth.

26
The Crown Jewel
Robert E. Cohen
August 7, 1999
Dedication: Deion Baldwin

The crown jewel is something that is
very precious. It is something of great
sentimental value. The crown jewel, which
is highly sought after, has the highest value
of any other stone. It is such a beautiful
sight that when everyone sees it they are so
amazed at the sight of it they will literally
sit there and stare at it for hours at a time.

27
The Unique Female
Robert E. Cohen
August 8, 1999
Dedication: Nikki Inge

The unique female is one who is very
popular. She is also a very educated
female. She is a fun loving female who is
a joy to be around. She is a very healthy
female who stays in good health all year
long. The unique female is very strong and
independent and does not depend on anyone
for anything. These are qualities of a real
intelligent female such as NIKKI INGE.

28
The Perfect Female
Robert E. Cohen
August 10, 1999

The perfect female is one who is very intelligent. She is also a very remarkable female who is very nice. However, she is one who plays hard to get because she knows that she can have any male that she chooses because she is just that beautiful. When she walks by all the boys, stop and stare at the tantalizing beauty of a true black female.

29
The African Specialty
Robert E. Cohen
September 12, 1999

The African Specialty is a very beautiful
female that is of African descendant.
She also is a very unique accent that
I enjoy hearing. There is something
about this African Specialty that has
me interested in her. I just cannot
seem to figure out what it is. There is
definitely something special about this
female that has me hypnotized and I am
interested in becoming friends with her.

30
The Spiritual Angel
Robert E. Cohen
December 16, 1999
Inspiration: Keisha Johnson

The Spiritual Angel is a very special angel that God only sent to perform special duties upon a perpendicular person. The angel is assigned to that one perpendicular person until their death. The Spiritual Angel is also one who understands the power of prayer and how prayer changes things. The Spiritual Angel's prayers are very strong detailed prayers so when the Spiritual Angel prays God knows exactly what the angel is asking for. When the Spiritual Angel asks for something it asks for supplication and God gets glorified that way.

31
The Mournful Tear
Robert E. Cohen
December 16, 1999

The mournful tear is a tear that is slightly
different from a regular tear. A regular tear
could be a tear for anything but a mournful
tear signifies a loss of something, usually
a family member or someone who is close
to you. Mournful tears are more extreme
because when you mourn (depending on the
person and how close you are) your mourning
period could take weeks, months, or even
years but never rush a grieving period.

32
The Blessing
Robert E. Cohen
January 2, 2000
Inspiration: Lawrissa Baker

Sometimes Gods puts certain things in
our lives that we may not understand why
He is doing it. For example, when you
first meet a person you do not realize it
but God could be trying to bless you.
On January 1, 2000 I met a friend that
I consider to be very special. Someone
that I feel I can express my feelings about
anything and it will not go any further.
Most people would think of that as just a
close friend. The reason I would consider
this friend a blessing is because this
person has really helped me to realize the
importance of having a real relationship
with the Lord and Savior, Jesus Christ.

33
The Friend
Robert E. Cohen
January 14, 2000

A friend is someone who you can go to about anything. It will remain confidential between you and that person. Once you and that person have developed a close relationship, you feel much more comfortable about opening up and expressing your feelings about anything.

34
The Heart of Gold
Big Rob
February 3, 2000

A person with a heart of gold is a person who is very kind-hearted. This person is someone who is very understanding and that you can confide in about anything and it will not go any further than you and that person. You and that person have developed that type of respect for one another.

35
Valentine
Big Rob
February 3, 2000

A Valentine is an extremely special person
that you care about deeply. When you
care for someone deeply at first, you
may not express your feelings to them
because you are not sure how the person
will react to your feelings towards them.

36
The Higher Power
Big Rob
February 7, 2000

The Higher Power is a power so strong
that when this powerful spirit touches
you it will be so powerful that when
you come in contact with it you will
instantly fall to the ground and be healed
because the higher power has so much
that all you would have to do is ask. The
Higher Power would give you whatever
you need if we just ask for assistance.

37
Reality
Robert E. Cohen
February 25, 2000

Reality is something that everyone at
one point or another we all have to face
whether we like it or not. Reality is also
something that depending on the person
that may have difficulty dealing with reality
but that is just the cruel part of life.

38
Strong Man
Robert E. Cohen
April 24, 2000

A strong man is a man who is very educated
and is full of wisdom and knowledge.
One who is very kind and trustworthy
and who is comfortable with himself.
He never acts shady when he is with
his woman and is very respectful.

39
Haters
Robert E. Cohen
May 10, 2000

Haters are people who are jealous of you
because you can get just about anything
they want including money and women.
When people see you getting a lot of
attention people who you think are your
friends begin to turn their backs on
you simply because they are jealous.

40
The Heart
Robert E. Cohen
May 12, 2000

The heart is something that is very strong
and compassionate and should not be
mistreated. However, if the unthinkable
should happen the person that does
the mistreating should be willing to
give a sincere apology. However, some
people do not believe in correcting
their wrongs and that is what causes a
lot of heartache and pain between two
people that vow to be inseparable.

41
My Heart
Big Rob
May 15, 2000
Dedication: Tiana Speight

My heart is a very special person who I
think is very cool. She is a very intelligent
female who I am very proud to be friends
with. The reason why I consider her to be
my heart is because every time I see her my
heart seems to skip a beat. I try really hard
not to show it but sometimes my feelings
overshadow my better judgment. That is
okay because I'd rather her know how I feel.

42
Prayer
Big Rob
May 27, 2000
Dedication: Renarda Tolbert

When people pray they have to be
very patient and have faith that God
will hear and answer your prayers. It
takes time for God to work out all the
pros and cons of your problems and
people have to be patient with God.

43
Thank You
Big Rob
June 9, 2000

Thank you for the day
Thank you for the night
Thank you for the darkness
Thank you for the light.
Thank you for the success that
you brought into my life.
Thank you for your mercy.
Thank you for you grace.
Thank you for the joy that
you bring upon my face.
Thank you for the love.
Thank you for the grace.
Thank you for how your word
spreads around a place.

44
Faith
Big Rob
June 9, 2000

Faith is something that as we Christians should have and most do. However, our faith is not always what it should be. When the devil begins to attack, we as Christians fall right into the devil's trap. We sometimes don't even realize it until the devil has already worked his way inside of us and tries to control our way of thinking. This is when you have to tell the devil no!! I will not live this way and that forward vow to live for the Lord and Savior Jesus Christ.

45
The Hurt in My Heart
Big Rob
June 12, 2000

The hurt in my heart is very painful because
sometimes I feel as if no one is interested
in what I have to say. Even though I don't
show it all the time someone ignores me I feel
hurt. But what hurts more than anything is
the fact that these are no strangers, it's my
own mother and twin sister. That's right, my
family. The two people who are suppose to
mean the most to me are the ones stabbing
me right in the back. I am really having
trouble trying to figure out how they could
be so cold hearted and still sleep comfortably
at night knowing what they are not treating
me the way that I deserve to be treated. They
think just because I am not able to do certain
things for myself that gives them the right
to disrespect me and expect me to just sit
there and take it with no response. As I try
to do that it does not always work because I
find it hard to be humble when someone is
disrespecting me for no apparent reason.
Example: When I ask for something to
drink they say wait a minute and it may
be another twenty minutes before I get it.
I have to ask repeatedly because either
they forget or they just don't care. Now
I should not feel that way but how can
not when that is what's really going on.

46
Disappointment and Hurt
Big Rob
June 13, 2000

In my heart lately all that I can feel is
disappointment and hurt. The reason for
it, well honestly, there is no reason except
for the fact that I am physically disabled
which limits the things that I am able to do
independently. This is a serious concern for
me because some things that I need are very
crucial for daily living. When I ask someone
in my family for something they are slow
about getting it for me and it makes me feel
as if I am talking to a brick wall. That is
what makes me feel all this disappointment
and hurt in my heart which at some point
is going to transform into just plain anger.
Before I end up directing my emotions in the
wrong place I try to avoid saying anything
to anybody. I don't want to appear to be
a heartless person because I am not that
type of person. It's very unfortunate that
I get treated better by outsiders than my
own family. This is where majority of my
disappointment and hurt comes from.
The person that most of my
disappointment and hurt is directed
towards is my mother. She never listens
to me and that hurts me deeply.

47
Dear God
June 13, 2000
Big Rob

Dear God,
My name is Robert E. Cohen and I am a seventeen year old who believes in Your word but right now I am experiencing some problems with my family. I know what You already know and I am asking for Your help and guidance to see me through these problems. Father God I realize that I cannot do it alone but with Your help I can do it because I can do all things through Christ that strengthens me. I know that my faith has not been what it should be but I am counting on You to make a metamorphic change in my life and help me to be a better person and be more Christ-like.

In Jesus name,
Amen

48
Loneliness
Big Rob
June 14, 2000

I consider myself to be a well rounded
person most of the time. I am happy and
satisfied with myself but lately I have not
been my normal high spirited, chipper
self. The reason why is simply because
I am going through some conflicts with
people who are very important to me and
it hurts me much. Sometimes I can't even
express myself to them because they won't
listen to me. It really hurts because it
makes me feel as if they don't care about
me and that is what makes me feel the
loneliness. However, I feel if they had to
be in my situation for twenty four hours
they would see me in a different way.

49
The Missing Piece
Big Rob
June 14, 2000

The missing piece in my life is a piece
that I feel is very important for me to feel
that my heart is filled with all the joy,
excitement, and inspiration that I feel is
necessary so that my heart will be fulfilled.
All the hurt and pain will be temporarily
forgotten. But the thing about this missing
piece is that it takes time to find. I need
to examine all the factors in finding this
missing piece to make sure that the piece
is special, caring, and kind. The missing
piece in my life is that special someone.

50
Tears of Sadness
Big Rob
June 15, 2000

I have tears of sadness because of what I am
going through. My tears of sadness are very
extreme and hurtful tears. These tears are
very unnecessary because I feel that if people
on the outside could see what was happening
on the inside they would understand why my
heart is filled with so much hurt and anger.
One reason for the hurt is because my
mother will not do certain things for me
and it really bothers me. She really does
not care how it affects me at all. Things
such as taking me somewhere every now
and then so that we can have some time
together. But she won't even do that.
Another reason why I have tears of sadness
is because I have yet to find that special
someone who I can talk to about anything,
someone who I can spend time with
and share unforgettable memories with,
and someone who does not mind being
seen with a person who has a disability.
Just because a person has a disability
does not mean there is anything wrong
with their mind. Most females see a
wheelchair and they automatically think
that there is something wrong with the
way I think. It is not fair because you
should never judge a book by its cover.

51
Cherish
Big Rob
June 19, 2000

To cherish something means that you
greatly appreciate the value. When you
cherish something you should not only
greatly appreciate it but you should also
keep it close to your heart and treat it
with the utmost respect. It is special and
in some cases it could be the only thing
that keeps you going from day to day.

52
He's There
Big Rob
June 19, 2000

When I am troubled, He's there.
When I am sick, He's there.
When I am hurt, He's there.
When I am disappointed, He's there.
When I overwhelmed with the
troubles of the world, He's there.
When I need a shoulder to cry on, He's there.
When I need someone who will listen to
me without interrupting, He's there.
When I just need someone to
confide in, He's there.

Yes, God is always there whenever I need
Him. He's always kind, compassionate,
and caring. Thank you for being so patient
and willing to help someone in need.

53
Wish
Big Rob
June 20, 2000

I wish for a better relationship
with my mother and sister.
I wish wisdom, knowledge,
and understanding.
I wish to be a better person in Christ.
I wish to be strong willed caring person
with a hunger for knowledge.
I wish to be a more obedient person.
I wish for joy, peace, and happiness.
I wish people would accept me as I am and
not judge me because of my condition.
I wish for a beautiful black woman who I can
express myself to without being criticized
by her, her family, and her friends.
I wish for a more prosperous
and joyful life on earth.

54
The Special Love
Robert E. Cohen
June 21, 2000

The special love is a very deep passionate love that is shared by two people who care about each other deeply. This love is a very kind compassionate love that people share when they have been together for a long time and have shared some unforgettable memories. Unfortunately, I have yet to find this special love. Hopefully, I will be fortunate enough to find her someday.

55
The Black Man
Big Rob
June 23, 2000

The black man is the type who is very strong
and high spirited. He has certain outstanding
qualities about himself which allows him
to stand out from everyone in the crowd. It
takes a strong willed and determined young
black male to meet these extremely high
standards. As a black male in today's society
it is extremely difficult for us to achieve
the things that we wish to achieve. A great
number of black males get caught up doing
things that they should not be doing and
end up behind bars and that temporarily
stops their education. Once they are released
the majority of black males don't make an
effort to return to school and continue their
education. That is why the job market lacks
black males and it's really their own fault. A
lot of things that we do as black males are
not necessary and they wonder why they are
not accepted by the world that we live in.

56
The Spiritual Inspiration
Big Rob
June 25, 2000

The spiritual inspiration is a strong
inspiration that can only come from above.
When God inspires you to do something
you should just go ahead and do it because
God may be trying to bless you. If you
don't follow up on it you could miss the
blessing that God has in store for you.
Today after I arrived at church before
exiting the bus I asked the driver to pray
with me because God placed it on my heart
a few weeks ago to ask this person to do
this. When the thought first came to me
I was a little afraid to ask for this request
because I was not sure how the person would
react. God told me to do it so I did and we
prayed. Prayer made me a lot stronger. I
also got some concerns off my chest.
This is my testimony about how God blesses
people without an extreme amount of work.

Your faithful servant,
Robert E. Cohen

57
The Love That a Brother Has for a Sister
Robert E. Cohen
June 30, 2000

When a brother has love for a sister he will
do anything within his power to get with
this sister because she is just that beautiful
and he is willing to do anything to get her.
When he has a conversation with her she
seems to be a nice girl. When you talk to
her about family and friends she is cool
because people are always around her.
When it comes to talking to her about her
and a possible relationship she begins to
trip. When you try to get her to hook you
up with someone else she starts to tell that
she likes you. When you admired her she
would not give you the time of day and
now you're confused about what to do.

58
Heart II
Robert E. Cohen
July 9, 2000

Heart of love
Heart of peace
Heart of joy
Heart of grief
Heart of disappointment
Heart of pain
Heart of confusion
Heart of obedience
Heart of sweetness
Heart of neatness
Heart of gladness
Heart of sadness
Heart of fear
Heart of protection
Heart of kindness
Heart of weakness
Heart of strong will
Heart of grace

59
A New Friend
Robert E. Cohen
July 11, 2000

A new friend is someone who you have just met. This is a person who you don't know much about yet as time goes on you will get to know more about each other. Hopefully, you and that person will become good friends and have a progressive future together.

60
The Mysterious Female
Robert E. Cohen
July 15, 2000

The mysterious female is a female that
you hear a lot of things about. You want
to believe them but because of previous
experiences with things that you have
heard it makes it kind of difficult for you
to believe what you hear. That is why it
is imperative that you and the person
set up a meeting with each other so both
of you can remove any doubt that either
of you may have about the other.

61
The Guardian Angel
Robert E. Cohen
September 21, 2000

The guardian angel is one of protection,
one who watches over you day and night.
The guardian angel is one of strength,
one who is more powerful than
anyone could ever imagine.
The guardian angel is one of understanding,
someone you can confide in about anything.
The guardian angel is caring, one
who does not treat a person different
because of their condition.
The guardian angel is one of knowledge,
one who is always eager to learn.
The guardian angel is one who is
very comfortable with themselves,
one who does not worry about what
other people think of them.
The guardian angel is very cultured, one
who likes being in different settings.
The guardian angel is kind,
one who is graceful.
The guardian angel is very strong, one
who is capable of handling anything.

62
The Interest
Robert E. Cohen
October 2, 2000
Dedication: Jennifer Shealey

The interest is something that is
constantly on your mind and no matter
how hard you try to shake the feeling
sometimes it is impossible for you to
forget. The feeling is so strong you
cannot easily forget. It is something you
have just acquired but sometimes things
just happen in such a quick manner
that there is no time for hesitation.
My interest is someone that I just
met, but I knew the first time I laid
eyes on the "Interest" there was
something extremely special about it.

63
Hurt
Robert E. Cohen
October 6, 2000

Hurt is something that everyone experiences
at some point in life but it is how you
handle your hurt that makes a difference.
When someone is hurt their emotions
seem to overshadow their better judgment.
This could mean trouble for anyone who
crosses this person's path especially if
they do not cope with hurt very well. You
must be cautious about how to approach a
person who is trying to cope with hurt.

64
The Secret Love
Big Rob
November 12, 2000
Dedication: Aisha Burke

The Secret Love is a very strong, deep, and compassionate love that one person has for another person. This feeling that you have for the other person is such a strong appreciative love that you are willing to do anything that you can to assist this person with whatever they may need assistance with.

66
A Brother's Wish
Big Rob
November 16, 2000

When a brother wishes for something he
will do whatever he feels necessary to
make the wish come true even if what it
takes may seem impossible to achieve.
But as long as you keep your head up and
you have faith in time your wish will come
true. The wish of a brother like me is to
acquire all the education and knowledge
that I possibly can to ensure that I get the
best job possible paying the most money.
Another wish that a brother like me has is
to find that one special person that makes
your day better every time you see her even
if you and the person don't necessarily
have a relationship going on. She could
just be an extremely special friend.

65
Wisdom
Big Rob
November 16, 2000

Willing
Intelligence
Superior
Determined
Organized
Mighty

67
Thank You II
Big Rob
November 17, 2000

Father in the name of Jesus, I pray that
You will bless me and the people I love
in a special way. Father, I pray that You
will look down upon us every hour of the
day and if there is anything in our hearts
that is not like you I ask that You remove
it right now in the name of Jesus. Father
God, I ask that You guide and protect
us in whatever we do. Father I want
to thank You for all the blessings that
You bestowed until this day and for the
blessings that You will bestow upon us in
the future. In Jesus name I pray, Amen.

68
Thanksgiving
Big Rob
November 23, 2000

Thanksgiving is a time to give thanks for
the things that God has blessed us with
until this day and for those things yet to
come. Everyone has been blessed in several
different ways. Some have been blessed
with good homes and families. Some have
been blessed with the ability to help those
who are in need. Others have been blessed
with the ability to give advice to the lost
and confused. Whatever God has blessed
us with we should be thankful for it

69
Admire
Big Rob
December 2, 2000
Dedication: Ashley Harrison

When you admire something it means that
you think a lot of it whether it's a possession
or a person. In my case, it is a person that
I am particularly fond of. She is kind of
quiet and laid back. She is a very helpful
girl with a great personality. She is very
comfortable with herself and communicates
well with others. She is very dependable
and reliable and always there when you
need her. She is just an overall nice girl
with a big heart. She is very special to me.

70
Homeboy
Big Rob
December 18, 2000
Dedication: The Late Travis Williams

Homeboy you're in Heaven now and since
your departure I have experienced a certain
amount of difficulty dealing with your
death. I really don't understand why. You
have been gone for more than a year but
when the accident first happened it was
not as much of a conflict as it has been
the past three months. For the past three
months I have not been able to really
focus on anything except you because
when you died it really tore me apart.

Rest In Peace Homeboy

71
The Lost Homeboy
Big Rob
December 29, 2000
Dedication: The Late Travis Williams

The loss of a homeboy can be a very difficult thing to deal with because you never know when it will hit you that the person is actually gone and you will never see that person again. When it does hit and you realize that all the good times that you and that person had are over. It may take a while for you to come to the realization but when it does it will hurt and may take months, even years, to overcome this very painful obstacle. My homeboy has been dead for over a year and I have yet to overcome his death.

72
Brother
Big Rob
January 8, 2001
Dedication: The Late Travis Williams

Brother, you left earth to go be with
your Father in Heaven. When you first
died it did not cause me as much of a
conflict as it is right now because there
is not a day that passes that you don't
cross my mind. Brother, you not only
left me but you left an empty space
in my heart reserved for memories of
you. Oh how I miss you and adore you
and hope to see you again someday.

73

The Heart, the Mind, and the Soul
Big Rob
February 1, 2001

The heart, mind, and soul are of vital importance to what happens in our everyday lives because they are constantly at work doing their respective jobs separately but together as a cohesive unit. If one of these components is not functioning properly it can cause serious problems for the person and people they come in contact with. So you must be careful about how you handle The Heart, The Mind, and The Soul.

The Hood March 19, 2001
74
The Hood
Big Rob
March 19, 2001

The hood can be a very dangerous place
to live in because the hood has constant
activity happening in it. Some of the things
that happen are calm and some things are
quite dangerous. If there is a group of people
just sitting outside on the porch drinking
and discussing the events of the day there
is not much danger. On the other hand, if
there were gun shots ringing out causing
ruckus there could be a serious problem.

75
Spring
Big Rob
April 2, 2001

Spring is a very beautiful time of year
because there are so many beautiful things
to see like flowers growing in our own
front yards, trees blooming around town,
and the feeling of love in the air. Spring is
also a time for rest and relaxation and fun
in the sun. During spring the beaches are
packed and filled with activities for people
of all ages (mainly college students). People
lay on the beach with radios and sun tan
lotion getting a tan, in the swimming pool
to cool themselves, or walking around the
beach talking to and meeting new people
of all shapes, sizes, backgrounds, and
cultures. No matter what your interpretation
of spring is make sure to have fun.

76
My Heart's Feelings
Robert E. Cohen
September 30, 2001

My heart's feelings are strong ones because
lately all that I have been thinking of
is a certain person, a person of female
persuasion, someone who I think highly of,
someone I consider to be extremely special,
someone who is considerate of others,
someone who is helpful, someone who is
quiet, someone who is a joy to be around,
someone who is easy to communicate
with, someone who has a pleasant attitude,
someone who is intelligent, someone who
is talented, someone who is kind-hearted,
someone who is strong willed, someone who
is determined, someone who is creative,
someone who is amazing, someone who
is timid, someone who is outstanding,
someone who has a great deal of potential,
someone who is caring, someone who is
exciting, someone who is understanding,
someone who would make a great role
model, someone who is beautiful, someone
who is always presentable, someone who
is organized, someone who is respectful,
a person who is loving, someone who is
sensitive to others feelings, someone who
is neat, someone who is educated, someone
who is eager, someone who is unique,
someone who is dignified, someone who is

desirable, someone who has an inquisitive personality, someone who is laid back.

Overall this person is a beautiful, kindhearted, and respectable person who I am delighted and consider it an honor and pleasure to be friends with.

77
The Scholar on Wheels
Robert E. Cohen
November 15, 2001

I, Robert E. Cohen, am "The Scholar on Wheels". I am an intelligent person who gives my best in everything I endeavor in. I am strong willed person who has worked very hard to be where I am today. Although I have a disability called cerebral palsy, it does not hinder me from achieving my long-term goals and aspirations. Some of my hobbies include meeting new people, interacting in the community, being creative, helping others, and writing poetry about my feelings and past experiences. I consider myself a leader and continuously strive to become a better person every day. One outstanding characteristic about me is that I love to pray and encourage others to do the same. I love to make new friends but am very careful about whom I choose to hang around with. Two of my strong beliefs are that discrimination is morally and politically wrong, and it is better to give than to receive. I detest being put down by those who think negative of me because of my disability. I wish that some people could see past the wheelchair and acknowledge my intelligence and loving spirit.

Overall, I think that I am a very positive thinker who does not allow the fact that I am in a wheelchair stop me from achieving my goals. I am very inspirational person and a great role model for other teenagers. I am a remarkable student and a great person all around.

78
When
Robert E. Cohen
September 15, 2002

When I think of His goodness I know
I've been set free. When I think of
all the violent acts happening today
I thank Him for paving my way.
When I think of how good He is to me I know
His grace and mercy will never leave me.
When I think of His understanding I
know He's always listening to me.
When I think of His power it
keeps me on a straight path.

79
Floetic Justice
Robert E. Cohen
September 28, 2002

Floetic Justice is the justice to express
one's self freely and expect that your
audience will listen and respect the opinions
of people who don't share the same. In
today's society, we are entitled to freedom
of speech and sometimes people say things
that other people may not necessarily agree
with or respect especially if the audience
members are of different cultures and
belief systems. Thus no matter what one
individual believes we as humans being
should be able to share ideas and options
amongst each other without a lot of friction.

80
The Understanding Type
Robert E. Cohen
December 6, 2003
Dedication: Calandra Blockman

The understanding type is a person who
understands you and the things that you go
through regardless of the situation. They
are always there to listen to or help you
in any way they can. These are the people
who you speak to about anything. I know
a few people who fit into this category
known as the Understanding Type.
To fully understand everything about
someone with a disability you must first
take time and talk to the person and get
to know them. Until you get to know the
person you won't know what the person
is capable of or what the two of you may
be able to learn from each other. This is
what I experienced earlier this week when
speaking with a friend about some issues
on my mind. She really understood me and
made me feel a lot better about what was
going on. I really value our friendship.

81
Righteous Living
Robert E. Cohen
November 8, 2004

Living a righteous life is a difficult and
sometimes discouraging thing to do. This
world we live in is a very cold and heartless
place where no one cares about anyone
else. Instead of everyone working together
to make the world a better place for the
generations that will follow, we are too busy
trying to out do each other. We do not take
the time to empower and encourage each
other. Sometimes that is all we need to
keep us going. However, with the way this
world is developing right now, it will be a
while before we evolve to the point where
we can empower and encourage each other.

82
Love and Appreciation
Robert E. Cohen
November 14, 2004

In order to love and appreciate someone
there are several qualities about the person
that can be distinguished as soon as you look
at the person. The first is a relationship with
God. When we look at this person we can
tell they have not just an ordinary one but
a very strong and special relationship that
can be from far and near on a daily basis.
The second is a strong feeling of confidence
that cannot be destroyed or diminished
by anyone or anything that attempts to
destroy her. No matter what, she always
has a bright smile on her face regardless
of what she may be experiencing at the
moment. Her door is always open to us
whether we need academic assistance or
just an encouraging word to get us through
the day. She is never too busy to assist us.
The third is a willing heart where all
her love comes from. She gives us an
opportunity to express ourselves willingly
without interrupting, whether it's
positive or negative. Her ears, as well as
her heart, are always open and that is
why the students love her so much.

Thanks for all the love you've shown us
throughout the years. We love you.

83
The Mental Death
Robert E. Cohen
November 28, 2004

When someone dies mentally it does not
mean that they are brain dead, it simply
means that they may be experiencing
something that has their attention so
diverted that it may affect their everyday
performance in achieving the tasks they
have to deal with successfully. If your mind
is preoccupied there is a great possibility
that you won't be at one hundred percent.

Right now I am personally experiencing a
mental death of my own. Lately I have been
feeling like the members of my immediate
family are turning against me. Every time I
attempt to achieve my goals that I feel would
assist me in having a more independent and
prosperous life. The life that both God and I feel
I should be living there is someone attacking
me and planting disturbing thoughts in my
mind attempting to destroy my dreams while
destroying me in the process. They never
listen or try to understand what may be going
through my mind. This is the most hurtful
feeling to me because I am a young man with
a disability and still have tons of dreams that
I want to fulfill before I leave this earth. If I
stray away from these negative influences
to achieve my dreams I will do just that.

84
The Ideal Friendship
Robert E. Cohen
March 17, 2006
Dedicated to a very special friend
whom I am glad I had the pleasure
of meeting, Jacquina Nicholson

My ideal friendship is one of extreme joy
because not only is this a great friendship
of communication it is also a great God
fearing friendship. We are both saved and we
are both good wholesome people who have
gotten along very well. This is probably the
most beautiful and exciting friendship I have
had in a long time. This is a friendship of
honesty, respect, kindness, and agape love.
We always have intelligent conversations
and laughter lasts for a long time. Even
though she is not ready for a relationship
right now, if nothing else, we can have a
beautiful friendship that could possibly
one day evolve into something more

85
Beautiful Friendship
Robert E. Cohen
August 3, 2009

The beautiful friendship that I have
is a special one because its one where
we connected almost instantly. The
conversations we have are on unexplainable
level. It's a friendship where both of us
watch out for each other and no matter what
there will be a unbreakable bond between us.
No matter what I need yours always there
how incredible it feels to know you care and
I will never take our friendship for granted.
I love you always keep you in my heart.

86
The Love of Friendship
January 22, 2008
Robert E. Cohen

The love of friendship is something that
is very special. When people experience
the love of friendship, it's something to be
respected and should never at any time be
treated with dishonor or distrust. It should
be treated with the utmost loyalty and
honor. It should be treated as a diamond
just out of the jewelry store. Just as a
new diamond leaves the store clean and
untouched, the love of friendship should
be treated in the same manner becuase
these days and times wholesome, healthy
friendship of this magnitude should be
treated as such, and you will be able to
experience the true love of friendship.

87
Soulmate
September 14, 2008
Robert E. Cohen
Dedication: Tiffany Joyce

My bestfriend who always has my back
no matter what happens in life and will
always have a special place in my heart
I love you and I'm praying for you.

A soulmate is someone in your life who
is very special to you. Someone who you
can depend on through thick and thin no
matter how rough things may seem they
will always be there for you and will never
turn there back on you. The person who I
consider to be my soulmate is someone who
I have had the pleasure of knowing for about
nine years even though we haven't been on
the soulmate level but a few months I feel
our bond becoming stronger each day even
though we don't communicate or see each
other as much as we would like too, it still
seems as if we are growing closer with each
passing day.I believe in her so much I would
go to the end of the earth with her if she
needed me too. She knows I love her and
would do anything in my power to assist her
with whatever she needs because I love her
just that much, because she's a real genuine
female and these days that is a very difficult
quality to find in a female, so I wouldn't

dare take our relationship for granted.

I love you with all my heart and always will.

The true poet,
Robert E. Cohen

88
Living The Dream
February 4, 2009
Robert E. Cohen

As we embark on the beginning of a
new year it's also a year full of changes
for America and its people because in
America on November 4, 2008 America
experienced a shift in power and also a
history making moment for the American
citizens, because we elected the first
African- American President. At that
moment I knew the change had come to
life, to see the historic occasion of what
Martin Luther King Jr. himself spoke of,
it was 44 years that came full circle at a
time when the world seemingly had been
turned on its ear and to live in America
right now. This triumph should allow us
as blacks to have faith and believe we can
achieve anything we set our minds too,
thus should begin to evaluate our lives
stop making excuses and go out and strive
for what we want out of our lives whether
it be a doctor, a lawyer, or a journalist. It
can be done. From Martin Luther King who
spoke it, to Barack Obama whos living it.

Celebrate our black history as it's made.
Robert E. Cohen

89
The Love in my Heart
August 4, 2008
Robert E. Cohen
Dedication: Tiffany Joyce

The love in my heart is a very special love to someone who I consider to be a great friend who is sweet, kind and caring. Someone who I can talk to about anything and don't have to worry about it going any further than the two of us. She is someone who over the past several months has shown me what it's like to have a true friend and the meaning of true friendship. Which is something I haven't had the pleasure in experiencing in a long time, and thats' something I will never forget as long as I live. Thank you for that. Someone I will always have love for no matter what happens.

I love you, always remember that.

90
Overcomer
September 29, 2009
Robert E. Cohen

The overcomer is someone who despite what obstacles comes their way the overcomer will always find a way to persist through them. I am the overcomer because over twenty seven years I have overcome several obstacles from being born with cerebral palsy to graduating from Savannah State University with a bachelor's degree in Sociology in December 2005 at the age of twenty three. In the process of this triumph, I had to deal with several obstacles from not having note takers to buildings not being to code ADA laws. That continued after graduation I ventured out to pursue a career. On March 26, 2006, God blessed me and I received my Ministers' license to preach the gospel as opportunity affords itself. In June 2006, God blessed me with my first job as a recreation leader for the city of Savannah Leisure Services Bureau. In January 2008 my career continued as a sales associate at Steve-n-Barry sports apparel store, which lasted approximately around 6 months. Currently I'm not in pursuit of a career in a way that God will be gloried because God has allowed me to overcome every obstacle placed before me up until this point. I am eternally grateful for that.

91
Patience
January 30, 2010
Robert E. Cohen

When people experience dry seasons,
they often find themselves becoming
discouraged with what they are attempting
to accomplish. During the journey from
college to finding a career, the preparation
period can be a trying one because once
a person completes all required courses,
the person believes that once they submit
resumes, they will be at the top of the
employer's hiring list. However, this is
hardly ever the case. I've had a four year
layoff between planting the seed and seeing
the harvest. So when you find yourself in
this season, don't be discouraged because
in the due season you shall reap. If you
faint not, then they that wait on the Lord
shall renew their strength. So hold on if you
are in a transitional season. God is going
to shower down blessing in your life if you
have faith the size of the mustard seed and
believe it will come to pass. Patience is a
virtue. Your faith determines your patience,
your patience determines your attitude, and
your attitude determines your aptitude.

92
Treasured Friendship
March 15, 2010
Robert E. Cohen

The treasured friendship is one that is extremely special and can be truly heart warming at times. When you have a treasured friendship you must treat it with the upmost respect and dignity because if it isn't, the treasured friendship will walk out and leave you lonely and miserable. So as much as possible live at peace with the treasured friendship.

93
Two hearts
Robert E. Cohen
April 18, 2010

Two hearts connected together as one by a
unexplainable bond that can never broken
any natural force on earth. This bond is
extremely special between people who are
open. Honest, and understanding of each
other feelings and respects each other point
of view whether or not they agree they
can and always will engage in intelligent.
Inspiring thought-provoking dialogue with
my closes friend next to God and my earthly
father. My best friend loves you. You will
always hold an extremely special place in
my heart as well as my life. Tiffany Joyce.

94
Honey
By:Robert E. Cohen
5/17/2010

Dedication Tiffany Joyce
My honey is someone who is sweet,
compassionate and kind. Someone who I love
dearly. Someone who I can connect with on
an intellual level. Someone who has both
of our best interest at heart. I love you.

ACKNOWLEDGEMENTS

1. The Lord
2. Robert and Gladys Cohen
3. The Delicate Flower inspired by Nikia Hall
4. The Crush dedicated to Dashawna Hanshaw
5. The spirit dedicated Sarah Truly
6. The Crown Jewel dedicated to Deion Baldwin
7. The Unique Female dedicated to Nikki Inge
8. The Spiritual Angel inspired by Keisha Johnson
9. The Blessing inspired by Lawrissa Baker
10. My Heart dedicated to Tiana Speight
11. Prayer dedicated to Renarda Tolbert
12. The Interest dedicated to Jennifer Shealey
13. The Secret Love dedicated to Aisha Burke
14. Admire dedicated to Ashley Harrison
15. Homeboy dedicated to the Late Travis Williams
16. The Lost Homeboy dedicated to the Late Travis Williams
17. Brother dedicated to the late Travis Williams
18. The Understanding Type dedicated to Calandra Blockman
19. The Ideal Friendship dedicated to a very special friend whom I am glad I had the pleasure of meeting Jacquina Nicholson
20. Soulmate dedicated to Tiffany Joyce
21. The Love In My Heart dedicated to Tiffany Joyce
22. The Beautiful Friendship Latanya Alston
23. Two Hearts dedicated to Tiffany Joyce

24. Charlene Flowers

25. Eureka Smith

26. Dr. Irvin Clark

27. Professor McCoy

28. Andrea Hatchett

29. James Morris III

30. Dicky Stone

31. Sunny Imgram

32. Brenda Hoskins

33. Elizabeth Hamilton

34. Bianca Bostic

35. Ashley Smith

36. Anthony & Felicia Williams

37. Ashley O'Bryan, Gretchen Perez & Tom Kohler

38. Shamonica McKinney

39. Pastor Whitherspoon, Alpha-Omega Worship Center

40. Georgia Eye Front desk staff